AMAZON CATEGORIES

RESOURCE FOR AUTHORS

Get your Book in the Right Category for Maximum Exposure

Compiled by Val Waldeck

www.valwaldeck.com

Reaching Our Generation One Book at a Time

Categories are vital to the success of your selling. That is a major way buyers find your books

> PLEASE NOTE: THESE CATEGORIES WERE
> CURRENT IN DECEMBER 2016
> THEY MAY HAVE CHANGED SO BE AWARE

To choose the best browse categories:

- **Be accurate.** Pick the most accurate categories based on the subject matter of your book.
- **Be specific.** It's better to choose specific categories instead of general ones. Customers looking for specific topics will more easily find your book, and Amazon will display your book in the general categories as well. For example, a book in the "FICTION > Fantasy > Historical" category will also show up in searches for general fiction and general fantasy books. Only select a "General" category if your book is actually a general book about a broad topic.
- **Be Concise.** Don't be redundant. Choosing even a single category will display your book in a variety of searches, so don't list your book in both a category and any or its sub-categories. For example, don't select both "FICTION > Fantasy > Historical" and "FICTION > Fantasy." Selecting one specific, accurate category is more effective than listing a redundant second category.
- **Note:** To list titles in the Children's or Teen & Young Adult categories on Amazon.com, Amazon.co.uk, and Amazon.de, you must select at least one Juvenile Category (BISAC Subject Code). For Children's categories, you'll also need to set the minimum recommended

reading age to 0 – 11 years old. For Teen & Young Adult categories on Amazon.com and Amazon.co.uk, set the minimum recommended reading age to 13 – 17 years old, and for Amazon.de, set the minimum recommended reading age to 12 – 15 years. On Amazon.com and Amazon.co.uk, titles with a Juvenile Category and a minimum recommended age of 12 may be categorized in Children's, Teens, or both depending on other information about the title.

IMPORTANT

AMAZON CATEGORIES WITH KEYWORD REQUIREMENTS

In order to ensure that Amazon places your books in the correct category, please check their Keyword requirements (Page 131).

TIP

Take your time choosing the right categories for your book. Amazon require at least two.

Drill down and select relevant sub-categories.

TABLE OF CONTENTS

AMAZON CATEGORIES

CATEGORIES FOR PUBLISHING KINDLE DIGITAL AND PAPERBACK BOOKS

FICTION

Fiction

General
Action & Adventure
African American

- General
- Christian
- Contemporary Women
- Erotica
- Historical
- Mystery & Detective
- Urban

Alternative History
Amish & Mennonite
Anthologies
Asian American
Biographical
Black Humor
Christian

- General
- Classic & Allegory
- Collections & Anthologies
- Fantasy
- Futuristic
- Historical

AMAZON CATEGORIES

- Romance
- Suspense
- Western

Classics
Coming of Age
Contemporary Women
Crime
Cultural Heritage
Dystopian
Erotica
Fairy Tales, Folk Tales, Legends & Mythology
Family Life
Fantasy

- General
- Collections & Anthologies
- Contemporary
- Dark Fantasy
- Epic
- Historical
- Paranormal
- Urban

Gay
Ghost
Gothic
Hispanic & Latino
Historical
Holidays
Horror
Humorous
Jewish
Legal
Lesbian
Literary
Magical Realism
Mashups
Media Tie-In

Medical
Mystery & Detective
- General
- Collections & Anthologies
- Cozy
- Hard-Boiled
- Historical
- International Mystery & Crime
- Police Procedural
- Private Investigators
- Traditional British
- Women Sleuths

Native American & Aboriginal
Noir
Occult & Supernatural
Political
Psychological
Religious
Romance
- General
- African American
- Collections & Anthologies
- Contemporary
- Erotica
- Fantasy
- Gay
- Historical
    - General
    - 20th Century
    - Ancient World
    - Medieval
    - Regency
    - Scottish
    - Victorian
    - Viking
- Lesbian

- Military
- Multicultural & Interracial
- New Adult
- Paranormal
- Romantic Comedy
- Science Fiction
- Suspense
- Time Travel
- Western

Sagas

Satire

Science Fiction

- General
- Action & Adventure
  - Alien Contact
  - Apocalyptic & Post-Apocalyptic
  - Collections & Anthologies
- Cyberpunk
- Genetic Engineering
- Hard Science Fiction
- Military
- Space Opera
- Steampunk
- Time Travel

Sea Stories

Short Stories

Sports

Superheroes

Thrillers

- General
- Crime
- Espionage
- Historical
- Legal
- Medical
- Military

- Political
- Supernatural
- Suspense
- Technological

Urban

Visionary & Metaphysical

War & Military

Westerns

Yaoi Light Novels

- General
- Boys' Love Novels

NON-FICTION

Antigues & Collectibles

General

Americana

Art

Autographs

Books

Bottles

Buttons & Pins

Canadian

Care & Restoration

Clocks & Watches

Coins, Currency & Medals

Comics

Dolls

Figurines

Firearms & Weapons

Furniture

Glass & Glassware

Jewelry

Kitchenware

Magazines & Newspapers

Military

Non-Sports Cards

Paper Ephemera

Performing Arts

Political

Popular Culture

Porcelain & China

Postcards

Posters

Pottery & Ceramics

Radios & Televisions

Records

Reference (CS General)

Rugs

Silver, Gold & Other Metals

Sports

Sports Cards

- General
- Baseball
- Basketball
- Football
- Hockey

Stamps

Teddy Bears

Textiles & Costume

Tobacco-Related

Toy Animals

Toys

Transportation

Wine

Architecture

General

Adaptive Reuse & Renovation
Annuals
Buildings
- General
- Landmarks & Monuments
- Public, Commercial & Industrial
- Religious
- Residential

Codes & Standards
Criticism
Decoration & Ornament
Design, Drafting, Drawing & Presentation
Historic Preservation
- General
- Restoration Techniques

History
- General
- Ancient & Classical
- Baroque & Rococo
- Contemporary
- Medieval
- Modern
- Prehistoric & Primitive
- Renaissance
- Romanticism

Individual Architects & Firms
- General
- Essays
- Monographs

Interior Design
- General
- Lighting
- Landscape

Methods & Materials
Professional Practice
Project Management

Reference
Regional
Security Design
Study & Teaching
Sustainability & Green Design
Urban & Land Use Planning

Art

General
African
American
- General
- African American
- Asian American
- Hispanic American

Annuals
Art & Politics
Asian
Australian & Oceanian
Body Art & Tattooing
Business Aspects
Canadian
Caribbean & Latin American
Ceramics
Collections, Catalogs, Exhibitions
- General
- Group Shows
- Permanent Collections

Color Theory
Conceptual
Conservation & Preservation
Criticism & Theory
Digital
European
Film & Video

Folk & Outsider Art

Graffiti & Street Art

History

- General
- Ancient & Classical
- Baroque & Rococo
- Contemporary
- Medieval
- Modern
- Prehistoric & Primitive
- Renaissance
- Romanticism

Individual Artists

- General
- Artists' Books
- Essays
- Monographs

Middle Eastern

Mixed Media

Museum Studies

Native American

Performance

Popular Culture

Prints

Reference

Russian & Former Soviet Union

Sculpture & Installation

Study & Teaching

Subjects & Themes

- General
- Erotica
- Human Figure
- Landscapes & Seascapes
- Plants & Animals
- Portraits
- Religious

Techniques
- General
- Acrylic Painting
- Airbrush
- Calligraphy
- Cartooning
- Color
- Drawing
- Life Drawing
- Oil Painting
- Painting
- Pastel Drawing
- Pen & Ink Drawing
- Pencil Drawing
- Printmaking
- Sculpting
- Watercolor Painting

Bibles

General
Christian Standard Bible
- General
- Children
- Devotional
- New Testament & Portions
- Reference
- Study
- Text
- Youth & Teen

Common English Bible
- General
- Children
- Devotional
- New Testament & Portions
- Reference

- Study
- Text
- Youth & Teen

Contemporary English Version

- General
- Children
- Devotional
- New Testament & Portions
- Reference
- Study
- Text
- Youth & Teen

English Standard Version

- General
- Children
- Devotional
- New Testament & Portions
- Reference
- Study
- Text
- Youth & Teen

God's Word

- General
- Children
- Devotional
- New Testament & Portions
- Reference
- Study
- Text
- Youth & Teen

International Children's Bible

- General
- Children
- Devotional
- New Testament & Portions
- Reference

- Study
- Text
- Youth & Teen

King James Version

- General
- Children
- Devotional
- New Testament & Portions
- Reference
- Study
- Text
- Youth & Teen

La Biblia de las Americas

- General
- Children
- Devotional
- New Testament & Portions
- Reference
- Study
- Text
- Youth & Teen

Multiple Translations

- General
- Children
- Devotional
- New Testament & Portions
- Reference
- Study
- Text
- Youth & Teen

New American Bible

- General
- Children
- Devotional
- New Testament & Portions
- Reference

- Study
- Text
- Youth & Teen

New American Standard Bible

- General
- Children
- Devotional
- New Testament & Portions
- Reference
- Study
- Text
- Youth & Teen

New Century Version

- General
- Children
- Devotional
- New Testament & Portions
- Reference
- Study
- Text
- Youth & Teen

New International Reader's Version

- General
- Children
- Devotional
- New Testament & Portions
- Reference
- Study
- Text
- Youth & Teen

New International Version

- General
- Children
- Devotional
- New Testament & Portions
- Reference

- Study
- Text
- Youth & Teen

New King James Version
- General
- Children
- Devotional
- New Testament & Portions
- Reference
- Study
- Text
- Youth & Teen

New Living Translation
- General
- Children
- Devotional
- New Testament & Portions
- Reference
- Study
- Text
- Youth & Teen

New Revised Standard Version
- General
- Children
- Devotional
- New Testament & Portions
- Reference
- Study
- Text
- Youth & Teen

Nueva Version International
- General
- Children
- Devotional
- New Testament & Portions
- Reference

- Study
- Text
- Youth & Teen

Other Translations
- General
- Children
- Devotional
- New Testament & Portions
- Reference
- Study
- Text
- Youth & Teen

Reina Valera
- General
- Children
- Devotional
- New Testament & Portions
- Reference
- Study
- Text
- Youth & Teen

The Message
- General
- Children
- Devotional
- New Testament & Portions
- Reference
- Study
- Text
- Youth & Teen

Today's New International Version
- General
- Children
- Devotional
- New Testament & Portions
- Reference

- Study
- Text
- Youth & Teen

Biography & Autobiography

General
Adventurers & Explorers
Artists, Architects, Photographers
Business
Composers & Musicians
Criminals & Outlaws
Culinary
Cultural Heritage
Editors, Journalists, Publishers
Educators
Entertainment & Performing Arts
Environmentalists & Naturalists
Historical
Law Enforcement
Lawyers & Judges
LGBT
Literary
Medical
Military
Native Americans
People with Disabilities
Personal Memoirs
Philosophers
Political
Presidents & Heads of State
Reference
Religious
Rich & Famous
Royalty
Science & Technology

Social Activists
Social Scientists & Psychologists
Sports
Women

Body, Mind & Spirit ✓

General
Afterlife & Reincarnation
Ancient Mysteries & Controversial Knowledge
Angels & Spirit Guides
Astrology
- General
- Eastern
- Horoscopes

Channeling & Mediumship
Crystals
Divination
- General
- Fortune Telling
- Palmistry
- Tarot

Dreams
Entheogens & Visionary Substances
Feng Shui
Gaia & Earth Energies
Healing
- General
- Energy
- Prayer & Spiritual

Hermetism & Rosicrucianism
I Ching
Inspiration & Personal Growth ✓
Magick Studies
Mindfulness & Meditation ✓
Mysticism

New Thought
Numerology
Occultism
Parapsychology
- General
- ESP
- Near-Death Experience
- Out-of-Body Experience

Prophecy
Reference
Sacred Sexuality
Shamanism
Spiritualism
Spirituality
- Celtic Spirituality
- Goddess Worship

Supernatural
UFOs & Extraterrestrials
Unexplained Phenomena
Witchcraft

Business & Economics

General
Accounting
- General
- Financial
- Governmental
- Managerial
- Standards

Advertising & Promotion
Auditing
Banks & Banking
Bookkeeping
Budgeting
Business Communication

- General
- Meetings & Presentations

Business Ethics

Business Etiquette

Business Law

Business Mathematics

Business Writing

Careers

- General
- Internships
- Job Hunting
- Resumes

Commerce

Commercial Policy

Conflict Resolution & Mediation

Consulting

Consumer Behavior

Corporate & Business History

Corporate Finance

- General
- Private Equity
- Valuation
- Venture Capital

Corporate Governance

Crowdfunding

Customer Relations

Decision-Making & Problem Solving

Development

- General
- Business Development
- Economic Development
- Sustainable Development

Distribution

E-Commerce

- General
- Auctions & Small Business

- Internet Marketing
- Online Trading

Econometrics

Economic Conditions

Economic History

Economics

- General
- Comparative
- Macroeconomics
- Microeconomics
- Theory

Education

Entrepreneurship

Environmental Economics

Exports & Imports

Facility Management

Finance

- General
- Financial Engineering
- Financial Risk Management
- Wealth Management

Forecasting

Foreign Exchange

Franchises

Free Enterprise

Government & Business

Green Business

Home-Based Businesses

Human Resources & Personnel Management

Industrial Management

Industries

- General
- Agribusiness
- Automobile Industry
- Computers & Information Technology
- Energy

- Entertainment
- Fashion & Textile Industry
- Financial Services
- Food Industry
- Hospitality, Travel & Tourism
- Manufacturing
- Media & Communications
- Natural Resource Extraction
- Park & Recreation Management
- Pharmaceutical & Biotechnology
- Retailing
- Service
- Transportation

Inflation
Information Management
Infrastructure
Insurance

- General
- Automobile
- Casualty
- Health
- Liability
- Life
- Property
- Risk Assessment & Management

Interest
International

- General
- Accounting
- Economics
- Marketing
- Taxation

Investments & Securities

- General
- Analysis & Trading Strategies
- Bonds

- Commodities
  - General
  - Energy
  - Metals
- Derivatives
- Futures
- Mutual Funds
- Options
- Portfolio Management
- Real Estate
- Stocks

Knowledge Capital

Labor

Leadership

Mail Order

Management

Management Science

Marketing
- General
- Direct
- Industrial
- Multilevel
- Research
- Telemarketing

Mentoring & Coaching

Mergers & Acquisitions

Money & Monetary Policy

Motivational

Museum Administration & Museology

Negotiating

New Business Enterprises

Nonprofit Organizations & Charities
- General
- Finance & Accounting
- Fundraising & Grants
- Management & Leadership

- Marketing & Communications

Office Automation
Office Equipment & Supplies
Office Management
Operations Research
Organizational Behavior
Organizational Development
Outsourcing
Personal Finance
- General
- Budgeting
- Investing
- Money Management
- Retirement Planning
- Taxation

Personal Success
Production & Operations Management
Project Management
Public Finance
Public Relations
Purchasing & Buying
Quality Control
Real Estate
- General
- Buying & Selling Homes
- Commercial
- Mortgages

Reference
Research & Development
Sales & Selling
- General
- Management

Secretarial Aids & Training
Skills
Small Business
Statistics

Strategic Planning
Structural Adjustment
Taxation
- General
- Corporate
- Small Business

Time Management
Total Quality Management
Training
Urban & Regional
Women in Business
Workplace Culture

Computers

General
Bioinformatics
Buyer's Guides
CAD-CAM
Calculators
CD-DVD Technology
Certification Guides
- General
- A+
- MCSE

Client-Server Computing
Compilers
Computer Engineering
Computer Graphics
Computer Literacy
Computer Science
Computer Simulation
Computer Vision & Pattern Recognition
Computerized Home & Entertainment
Cybernetics
Data Modeling & Design

Data Processing

Data Transmission Systems

- General
- Broadband
- Electronic Data Interchange
- Wireless

Data Visualization

Databases

- General
- Data Mining
- Data Warehousing
- Servers

Desktop Applications

- General
- Databases
- Design & Graphics
- Desktop Publishing
- Email Clients
- Personal Finance Applications
- Presentation Software
- Project Management Software
- Spreadsheets
- Suites
- Word Processing

Digital Media

- General
- Audio
- Photography
- Video & Animation

Document Management

Documentation & Technical Writing

Educational Software

Electronic Commerce

Electronic Publishing

Enterprise Applications

- General

- Business Intelligence Tools
- Collaboration Software

Expert Systems

Hardware

- General
- Mainframes & Minicomputers
- Mobile Devices
- Peripherals
- Personal Computers
  - General
  - Macintosh
  - PCs
  - Tablets

History

Image Processing

Information Technology

Information Theory

Intelligence (AI) & Semantics

Interactive & Multimedia

Internet

- General
- Application Development

Keyboarding

Logic Design

Machine Theory

Management Information Systems

Mathematical & Statistical Software

Microprocessors

Natural Language Processing

Networking

- General
- Hardware
- Intranets & Extranets
- Local Area Networks
- Network Protocols
- Vendor Specific

Neural Networks

Online Services

Operating Systems

- General
- DOS
- Linux
- Macintosh
- Mainframe & Midrange
- UNIX
- Virtualization
- Windows Desktop
- Windows Server

Optical Data Processing

Programming

- General
- Algorithms
- Games
- Macintosh
- Microsoft
- Mobile Devices
- Object Oriented
- Open Source
- Parallel

Programming Languages

- General
- Ada
- ASP.NET
- Assembly Language
- BASIC
- C
- C#
- C++
- COBOL
- FORTRAN
- HTML
- Java

- JavaScript
- LISP
- Pascal
- Perl
- PHP
- Prolog
- Python
- RPG
- Ruby
- SQL
- UML
- VBScript
- Visual BASIC
- XML

Reference
Security

- General
- Cryptography
- Networking
- Online Safety & Privacy
- Viruses & Malware

Social Aspects

- General
- Human-Computer Interaction

Software Development & Engineering

- General
- Project Management
- Quality Assurance & Testing
- Systems Analysis & Design
- Tools

Speech & Audio Processing
System Administration

- General
- Disaster & Recovery
- Email Administration
- Linux & UNIX Administration

- Storage & Retrieval
- Windows Administration

Systems Architecture

- General
- Distributed Systems & Computing

User Interfaces

Utilities

Virtual Worlds

Web

- General
- Blogs
- Browsers
- Content Management Systems
- Design
- Podcasting & Webcasting
- Search Engines
- Site Directories
- Social Networking
- User Generated Content
- Web Programming
- Web Services & APIs

Cooking

General

Baby Food

Beverages

- General
- Bartending
- Beer
- Coffee & Tea
- Non-Alcoholic
- Wine & Spirits

Courses & Dishes

- General
- Appetizers

AMAZON CATEGORIES

- Bread
- Breakfast
- Brunch
- Cakes
- Casseroles
- Chocolate
- Confectionery
- Cookies
- Desserts
- Pastry
- Pies
- Pizza
- Salads
- Sauces & Dressings
- Soups & Stews

Entertaining
Essays & Narratives
Health & Healing

- General
- Allergy
- Cancer
- Diabetic & Sugar-Free
- Gluten-Free
- Heart
- High Protein
- Low Carbohydrate
- Low Cholesterol
- Low Fat
- Low Salt
- Weight Control

History
Holiday
Individual Chefs & Restaurants
Methods

- General
- Baking

- Barbecue & Grilling
- Canning & Preserving
- Cookery for One
- Frying
- Garnishing & Food Presentation
- Gourmet
- Low Budget
- Microwave
- Outdoor
- Professional
- Quantity
- Quick & Easy
- Raw Food
- Slow Cooking
- Special Appliances
- Wok

Pet Food
Reference
Regional & Ethnic
- General
- African
- American
    - General
    - California Style
    - Middle Atlantic States
    - Middle Western States
    - New England
    - Northwestern States
    - Southern States
    - Southwestern States
    - Western States
- Asian
- Cajun & Creole
- Canadian
- Caribbean & West Indian
- Central American & South American

- Chinese
- English, Scottish & Welsh
- European
- French
- German
- Greek
- Hungarian
- Indian & South Asian
- International
- Irish
- Italian
- Japanese
- Jewish & Kosher
- Mediterranean
- Mexican
- Middle Eastern
- Native American
- Pacific Rim
- Polish
- Portuguese
- Russian
- Scandinavian
- Soul Food
- Spanish
- Thai
- Turkish
- Vietnamese

Seasonal

Specific Ingredients

- General
- Dairy
- Fruit
- Game
- Herbs, Spices, Condiments
- Meat
- Natural Foods

- Pasta
- Poultry
- Rice & Grains
- Seafood
- Vegetables

Tablesetting

Vegetarian & Vegan

Crafts & Hobbies

General

Applique

Baskets

Beadwork

Book Printing & Binding

Candle & Soap Making

Carving

Crafts for Children

Decorating

Dollhouses

Dolls & Doll Clothing

Dough

Dye

Fashion

Flower Arranging

Folkcrafts

Framing

Glass & Glassware

Jewelry

Knots, Macrame & Rope Work

Leatherwork

Metal Work

Miniatures

Mixed Media

Model Railroading

Models

Nature Crafts

Needlework

- General
- Crocheting
- Cross-Stitch
- Embroidery
- Knitting
- Lace & Tatting
- Needlepoint

Origami

Painting

Papercrafts

Patchwork

Polymer Clay

Potpourri

Pottery & Ceramics

Printmaking

Puppets & Puppetry

Quilts & Quilting

Reference

Ribbon Work

Rugs

Scrapbooking

Seasonal

Sewing

Stenciling

Stuffed Animals

Toymaking

Weaving

Wirework

Wood Toys

Woodwork

Design

General

Book
Clip Art
Decorative Arts
Essays
Fashion
Furniture
Graphic Arts
- General
- Advertising
- Branding & Logo Design
- Commercial & Corporate
- Illustration
- Typography
History & Criticism
Industrial
Interior Decorating
Product
Reference
Textile & Costume

Drama

General
African
American
- General
- African American
Ancient & Classical
Anthologies
Asian
- General
- Japanese
Australian & Oceanian
Canadian
Caribbean & Latin American
European

- General
- English, Irish, Scottish, Welsh
- French
- German
- Italian
- Spanish & Portuguese

LGBT

Medieval

Middle Eastern

Religious & Liturgical

Russian & Former Soviet Union

Shakespeare

Women Authors

Family & Relationships

General

Abuse

- General
- Child Abuse
- Domestic Partner Abuse
- Elder Abuse

Activities

Adoption & Fostering

Alternative Family

Anger

Attention Deficit Disorder

Autism Spectrum Disorders

Baby Names

Babysitting, Day Care & Child Care

Bullying

Children with Special Needs

Conflict Resolution

Dating

Death, Grief, Bereavement

Divorce & Separation

Dysfunctional Families
Education
Eldercare
Extended Family
Friendship
Learning Disabilities
Life Stages
- General
- Adolescence
- Infants & Toddlers
- Mid-Life
- School Age
- Teenagers

Love & Romance
Marriage & Long Term Relationships
Military Families
Parenting
- General
- Fatherhood
- Grandparenting
- Motherhood
- Parent & Adult Child
- Single Parent
- Stepparenting

Peer Pressure
Prejudice
Reference
Siblings
Toilet Training

Games

General
Backgammon
Board
Card Games

- General
- Blackjack
- Bridge
- Poker
- Solitaire

Checkers

Chess

Crosswords

- General
- Dictionaries

Fantasy Sports

Gambling

- General
- Lotteries
- Sports
- Table
- Track Betting

Logic & Brain Teasers

Magic

Optical Illusions

Puzzles

Quizzes

Reference

Role Playing & Fantasy

Sudoku

Travel Games

Trivia

Video & Electronic

Word & Word Search

Gardening

General

Climatic

- General
- Desert

- Temperate
- Tropical

Container

Essays & Narratives

Flowers

- General
- Annuals
- Bulbs
- Orchids
- Perennials
- Roses
- Wildflowers

Fruit

Garden Design

Garden Furnishings

Greenhouses

Herbs

House Plants & Indoor

Japanese Gardens

Landscape

Lawns

Organic

Ornamental Plants

Reference

Regional

- General
- Canada
- Middle Atlantic
- Midwest
- New England
- Pacific Northwest
- South
- Southwest
- West

Shade

Shrubs

Techniques
Topiary
Trees
Urban
Vegetables

Health & Fitness

General
Acupressure & Acupuncture
Aerobics
Allergies
Alternative Therapies
Aromatherapy
Beauty & Grooming
Body Cleansing & Detoxification
Breastfeeding
Children's Health
Diet & Nutrition
- General
- Diets
- Food Content Guides
- Macrobiotics
- Nutrition
- Vitamins
- Weight Loss

Diseases
- General
- AIDS & HIV
- Alzheimer's & Dementia
- Cancer
- Chronic Fatigue Syndrome
- Contagious
- Diabetes
- Gastrointestinal
- Genetic

- Genitourinary & STDs
- Heart
- Immune & Autoimmune
- Musculoskeletal
- Nervous System
- Respiratory
- Skin

Endocrine System
Exercise
First Aid
Healing
Health Care Issues
Healthy Living
Hearing & Speech
Herbal Medications
Holism
Homeopathy
Infertility
Massage & Reflexotherapy
Men's Health
Naturopathy
Oral Health
Pain Management
Physical Impairments
Pregnancy & Childbirth
Reference
Safety
Sexuality
Sleep & Sleep Disorders
Vision
Women's Health
Work-Related Health
Yoga

History

General
Africa

- General
- Central
- East
- North
- South
    - General
    - Republic of South Africa
- West

Americas
Ancient

- General
- Egypt
- Greece
- Rome

Asia

- General
- Central Asia
- China
- India & South Asia
- Japan
- Korea
- Southeast Asia

Australia & New Zealand
Canada

- General
- Post-Confederation
- Pre-Confederation

Caribbean & West Indies
General
Cuba
Civilization
Essays

Europe
- General
- Austria & Hungary
- Baltic States
- Eastern
- Former Soviet Republics
- France
- Germany
- Great Britain
- Greece
- Ireland
- Italy
- Russia & the Former Soviet Union
- Scandinavia
- Spain & Portugal
- Western

Expeditions & Discoveries

Historical Geography

Historiography

Holocaust

Jewish

Latin America
- General
- Central America
- Mexico
- South America

Medieval

Middle East
- General
- Arabian Peninsula
- Egypt
- Iran
- Iraq
- Israel & Palestine
- Turkey & Ottoman Empire

Military

- General
- Afghan War
- Aviation
- Biological & Chemical Warfare
- Canada
- Iraq War
- Korean War
- Naval
- Nuclear Warfare
- Other
- Persian Gulf War
- Pictorial
- Special Forces
- Strategy
- United States
- Veterans
- Vietnam War
- Weapons
- World War I
- World War II

Modern

- General
- 16th Century
- 17th Century
- 18th Century
- 19th Century
- 20th Century
- 21st Century

Native American
North America
Oceania
Polar Regions
Reference
Renaissance
Revolutionary
Social History

Study & Teaching
United States

- General
- 19th Century
- 20th Century
- 21st Century
- Civil War Period
- Colonial Period
- Revolutionary Period
- State & Local
  - General
  - Middle Atlantic
  - Midwest
  - New England
  - Pacific Northwest
  - South
  - Southwest
  - West

World

House & Home

General
Cleaning, Caretaking & Organizing
Decorating
Design & Construction
Do-It-Yourself

- General
- Carpentry
- Electrical
- Masonry
- Plumbing

Equipment, Appliances & Supplies
Furniture
Hand Tools
House Plans

Outdoor & Recreational Areas
Power Tools
Reference
Remodeling & Renovation
Repair
Security
Sustainable Living
Woodworking

Humor

General
Form

- Anecdotes & Quotations
- Comic Strips & Cartoons
- Essays
- Jokes & Riddles
- Limericks & Verse
- Parodies
- Pictorial
- Puns & Word Play
- Trivia

Topic

- Adult
- Animals
- Business & Professional
- Language
- Marriage & Family
- Political
- Relationships
- Religion
- Sports

Language Arts & Discipline

General
Alphabets & Writing Systems

AMAZON CATEGORIES

Authorship
Communication Studies
Composition & Creative Writing
Editing & Proofreading
Grammar & Punctuation
Handwriting
Journalism
Lexicography
Library & Information Science
- General
- Administration & Management
- Archives & Special Libraries
- Cataloging & Classification
- Collection Development
- Digital & Online Resources
- School Media

Linguistics
- General
- Etymology
- Historical & Comparative
- Morphology
- Phonetics & Phonology
- Pragmatics
- Psycholinguistics
- Semantics
- Sociolinguistics
- Syntax

Literacy
Public Speaking
Publishing
Readers
Reading Skills
Reference
Rhetoric
Sign Language
Speech

Spelling
Study & Teaching
Style Manuals
Translating & Interpreting
Vocabulary

Law
General
Administrative Law & Regulatory Practice
Agricultural
Air & Space
Alternative Dispute Resolution
Annotations & Citations
Antitrust
Arbitration, Negotiation, Mediation
Banking
Bankruptcy & Insolvency
Business & Financial
Child Advocacy
Civil Law
Civil Procedure
Civil Rights
Commercial
- General
- International Trade

Common
Communications
Comparative
Computer & Internet
Conflict of Laws
Constitutional
Construction
Consumer
Contracts
Corporate
Court Records

AMAZON CATEGORIES

Court Rules

Courts

Criminal Law

- General
- Juvenile Offenders
- Sentencing

Criminal Procedure

Customary

Defamation

Depositions

Dictionaries & Terminology

Disability

Discrimination

Educational Law & Legislation

Elder Law

Election Law

Emigration & Immigration

Entertainment

Environmental

Essays

Estates & Trusts

Ethics & Professional Responsibility

Evidence

Family Law

- General
- Children
- Divorce & Separation
- Marriage

Forensic Science

Gender & the Law

General Practice

Government

- General
- Federal
- State, Provincial & Municipal

Health

Housing & Urban Development

Indigenous Peoples

Insurance

Intellectual Property

- General
- Copyright
- Patent
- Trademark

International

Judicial Power

Jurisprudence

Jury

Labor & Employment

Land Use

Landlord & Tenant

Law Office Management

Legal Education

Legal History

Legal Profession

Legal Services

Legal Writing

Liability

Litigation

Living Trusts

Malpractice

Maritime

Media & the Law

Medical Law & Legislation

Mental Health

Mergers & Acquisitions

Military

Natural Law

Natural Resources

Paralegals & Paralegalism

Pension Law

Personal Injury

Practical Guides
Privacy
Property
Public
Public Contract
Public Utilities
Real Estate
Reference
Remedies & Damages
Research
Right to Die
Science & Technology
Securities
Sports
Taxation
Torts
Transportation
Trial Practice
Wills
Witnesses

Literary Criticism

General
African
American

- General
- African American
- Asian American
- Hispanic American

Ancient & Classical
Asian

- General
- Chinese
- Indic
- Japanese

- General
- Japanese Literature

Australian & Oceanian

Books & Reading

Canadian

Caribbean & Latin American

Children's Literature

Comics & Graphic Novels

Comparative Literature

Drama

European

- General
- Eastern
- English, Irish, Scottish, Welsh
- French
- German
- Italian
- Scandinavian
- Spanish & Portuguese

Fairy Tales, Folk Tales, Legends &   Mythology

Feminist

Gothic & Romance

Horror & Supernatural

Humor

Jewish

LGBT

Medieval

Middle Eastern

Mystery & Detective

Native American

Poetry

Reference

Renaissance

Russian & Former Soviet Union

Science Fiction & Fantasy

Semiotics & Theory

Shakespeare
Short Stories
Women Authors

Mathematics

General
Algebra

- General
- Abstract
- Elementary
- Intermediate
- Linear

Applied
Arithmetic
Calculus
Combinatorics
Complex Analysis
Counting & Numeration
Differential Equations

- General
- Ordinary
- Partial

Discrete Mathematics
Essays
Finite Mathematics
Functional Analysis
Game Theory
Geometry

- General
- Algebraic
- Analytic
- Differential
- Non-Euclidean

Graphic Methods
Group Theory

History & Philosophy
Infinity
Linear & Nonlinear Programming
Logic
Mathematical Analysis
Matrices
Measurement
Number Systems
Number Theory
Numerical Analysis
Optimization
Pre-Calculus
Probability & Statistics
- General
- Bayesian Analysis
- Multivariate Analysis
- Regression Analysis
- Stochastic Processes
- Time Series
Recreations & Games
Reference
Research
Set Theory
Study & Teaching
Topology
Transformations
Trigonometry
Vector Analysis

Medical

General
Acupuncture
Administration
AIDS & HIV
Allied Health Services

- General
- Emergency Medical Services
- Hypnotherapy
- Massage Therapy
- Medical Assistants
- Medical Technology
- Occupational Therapy
- Physical Therapy
- Radiological & Ultrasound Technology
- Respiratory Therapy

Alternative & Complementary Medicine

Anatomy

Anesthesiology

Atlases

Audiology & Speech Pathology

Bariatrics

Biochemistry

Biostatistics

Biotechnology

Cardiology

Caregiving

Chemotherapy

Chiropractic

Clinical Medicine

Critical Care

Dentistry

- General
- Dental Assisting
- Dental Hygiene
- Dental Implants
- Endodontics
- Oral Surgery
- Orthodontics
- Periodontics
- Practice Management
- Prosthodontics

AMAZON CATEGORIES

Dermatology

Diagnosis

Diagnostic Imaging

Dictionaries & Terminology

Diet Therapy

Diseases

Drug Guides

Education & Training

Embryology

Emergency Medicine

Endocrinology & Metabolism

Epidemiology

Essays

Ethics

Evidence-Based Medicine

Family & General Practice

Forensic Medicine

Gastroenterology

Genetics

Geriatrics

Gynecology & Obstetrics

Healing

Health Care Delivery

Health Policy

Health Risk Assessment

Hematology

Hepatology

Histology

History

Holistic Medicine

Home Care

Hospital Administration & Care

Immunology

Infection Control

Infectious Diseases

Instruments & Supplies

Internal Medicine
Laboratory Medicine
Lasers in Medicine
Long-Term Care
Medicaid & Medicare
Medical History & Records
Mental Health
Microbiology
Nephrology
Neurology
Neuroscience
Nosology
Nursing

- General
- Anesthesia
- Assessment & Diagnosis
- Critical & Intensive Care
- Emergency
- Fundamentals & Skills
- Gerontology
- Home & Community Care
- Issues
- LPN & LVN
- Management & Leadership
- Maternity, Perinatal, Women's Health
- Medical & Surgical
- Mental Health
- Nurse & Patient
- Nutrition
- Oncology & Cancer
- Pediatric & Neonatal
- Pharmacology
- Psychiatric
- Reference
- Research & Theory
- Test Preparation & Review

Nursing Home Care
Nutrition
Occupational & Industrial Medicine
Oncology
Ophthalmology
Optometry
Orthopedics
Osteopathy
Otorhinolaryngology
Pain Medicine
Parasitology
Pathology
Pathophysiology
Pediatric Emergencies
Pediatrics
Perinatology & Neonatology
Pharmacology
Pharmacy
Physical Medicine & Rehabilitation
Physician & Patient
Physicians
Physiology
Podiatry
Practice Management & Reimbursement
Preventive Medicine
Prosthesis
Psychiatry
- General
- Child & Adolescent
- Psychopharmacology

Public Health
Pulmonary & Thoracic Medicine
Radiology & Nuclear Medicine
Reference
Reproductive Medicine & Technology
Research

Rheumatology
Sports Medicine
Surgery
- General
- Colon & Rectal
- Laparoscopic & Robotic
- Neurosurgery
- Oral & Maxillofacial
- Plastic & Cosmetic
- Thoracic
- Transplant
- Vascular

Terminal Care
Test Preparation & Review
Toxicology
Transportation
Tropical Medicine
Ultrasonography
Urology
Veterinary Medicine
- General
- Equine
- Food Animal
- Small Animal

Music

General
Business Aspects
Discography & Buyer's Guides
Ethnic
Ethnomusicology
Genres & Styles
- General
- Ballet
- Big Band & Swing

AMAZON CATEGORIES

- Blues
- Chamber
- Children's
- Choral
- Classical
- Country & Bluegrass
- Dance
- Electronic
- Folk & Traditional
- Heavy Metal
- International
- Jazz
- Latin
- Military & Marches
- Musicals
- New Age
- Opera
- Pop Vocal
- Punk
- Rap & Hip Hop
- Reggae
- Rock
- Soul & R 'n B

History & Criticism
Individual Composer & Musician
Instruction & Study

- General
- Appreciation
- Composition
- Conducting
- Exercises
- Songwriting
- Techniques
- Theory
- Voice
- Lyrics

Musical Instruments
- General
- Brass
- Guitar
- Percussion
- Piano & Keyboard
- Strings
- Woodwinds

Printed Music
- General
- Artist Specific
- Band & Orchestra
- Brass
- Choral
- Guitar & Fretted Instruments
- Mixed Collections
- Musicals, Film & TV
- Opera & Classical Scores
- Percussion
- Piano & Keyboard Repertoire
- Piano-Vocal-Guitar
- Strings
- Vocal
- Woodwinds

Recording & Reproduction

Reference

Religious
- General
- Christian
- Contemporary Christian
- Gospel
- Hymns
- Jewish
- Muslim

Nature

General
Animal Rights
Animals

- General
- Bears
- Big Cats
- Birds
- Butterflies & Moths
- Dinosaurs & Prehistoric Creatures
- Fish
- Horses
- Insects & Spiders
- Mammals
- Marine Life
- Primates
- Reptiles & Amphibians
- Wildlife
- Wolves

Birdwatching Guides
Earthquakes & Volcanoes
Ecology
Ecosystems & Habitats

- General
- Coastal Regions & Shorelines
- Deserts
- Forests & Rainforests
- Lakes, Ponds & Swamps
- Mountains
- Oceans & Seas
- Plains & Prairies
- Polar Regions
- Rivers
- Wilderness

Endangered Species

Environmental Conservation & Protection
Essays
Fossils
Natural Disasters
Natural Resources
Plants
- General
- Aquatic
- Cacti & Succulents
- Flowers
- Mushrooms
- Trees

Reference
Regional
Rocks & Minerals
Seashells
Seasons
Sky Observation
Weather

Performing Arts

General
Acting & Auditioning
Animation
Business Aspects
Circus
Comedy
Dance
- General
- Ballroom
- Choreography & Dance Notation
- Classical & Ballet
- Folk
- History & Criticism
- Jazz

- Modern
- Popular
- Reference
- Tap

Film & Video

- General
- Direction & Production
- Guides & Reviews
- History & Criticism
- Reference
- Screenwriting

Individual Director

Monologues & Scenes

Puppets & Puppetry

Radio

- General
- History & Criticism
- Reference

Reference

Screenplays

Storytelling

Television

- General
- Direction & Production
- Guides & Reviews
- History & Criticism
- Reference
- Screenwriting

Theater

- General
- Broadway & Musical Revue
- Direction & Production
- History & Criticism
- Miming
- Playwriting
- Stagecraft

Pets

General
Birds
Cats
- General
- Breeds

Dogs
- General
- Breeds
- Training

Essays & Narratives
Fish & Aquariums
Food & Nutrition
Horses
Rabbits, Mice, Hamsters, Guinea Pigs, etc.
Reference
Reptiles, Amphibians & Terrariums

Philosophy

General
Aesthetics
Buddhist
Criticism
Eastern
Epistemology
Essays
Ethics & Moral Philosophy
Free Will & Determinism
Good & Evil
Hermeneutics
Hindu
History & Surveys
- General
- Ancient & Classical
- Medieval

- Modern
- Renaissance

Language

Logic

Metaphysics

Methodology

Mind & Body

Movements

- General
- Analytic
- Critical Theory
- Deconstruction
- Empiricism
- Existentialism
- Humanism
- Idealism
- Phenomenology
- Post-Structuralism
- Pragmatism
- Rationalism
- Realism
- Structuralism
- Utilitarianism

Political

Reference

Religious

Social

Taoist

Zen

Photography

General

Annuals

Business Aspects

Collections, Catalogs, Exhibitions

- General
- Group Shows
- Permanent Collections

Commercial

Criticism

History

Individual Photographers

- General
- Artists' Books
- Essays
- Monographs

Photoessays & Documentaries

Photojournalism

Reference

Subjects & Themes

- General
- Aerial
- Architectural & Industrial
- Celebrations & Events
- Celebrity
  - General
  - Celebrity Photo Books
- Children
- Erotica
- Fashion
- Historical
- Landscapes
- Lifestyles
- Nudes
- Plants & Animals
- Portraits
- Regional
- Sports

Techniques

- General
- Cinematography & Videography

- Color
- Darkroom
- Digital
- Equipment
- Lighting

Poetry

General

African

American

- General
- African American
- Asian American
- Hispanic American

Ancient & Classical

Anthologies

Asian

- General
- Chinese
- Japanese

Australian & Oceanian

Canadian

Caribbean & Latin American

Epic

European

- General
- English, Irish, Scottish, Welsh
- French
- German
- Italian
- Spanish & Portuguese

Gay & Lesbian

Medieval

Middle Eastern

Native American

Russian & Former Soviet Union
Subjects & Themes
- General
- Death, Grief, Loss
- Family
- Inspirational & Religious
- Love
- Nature
- Places

Women Authors

Political Science

General
American Government
- General
- Executive Branch
- Judicial Branch
- Legislative Branch
- Local
- National
- State

Censorship
Civics & Citizenship
Civil Rights
Colonialism & Post-Colonialism
Commentary & Opinion
Comparative Politics
Constitutions
Essays
Genocide & War Crimes
Geopolitics
Globalization
History & Theory
Human Rights
Imperialism

Intelligence & Espionage
Intergovernmental Organizations
International Relations
- General
- Arms Control
- Diplomacy
- Trade & Tariffs
- Treaties

Labor & Industrial Relations
Law Enforcement
NGOs
Peace
Political Economy
Political Freedom
Political Ideologies
- General
- Anarchism
- Communism, Post-Communism & Socialism
- Conservatism & Liberalism
- Democracy
- Fascism & Totalitarianism
- Nationalism & Patriotism
- Radicalism

Political Process
- General
- Elections
- Leadership
- Political Advocacy
- Political Parties

Propaganda
Public Affairs & Administration
Public Policy
- General
- City Planning & Urban Development
- Communication Policy
- Cultural Policy

- Economic Policy
- Environmental Policy
- Regional Planning
- Science & Technology Policy
- Social Policy
- Social Security
- Social Services & Welfare

Reference

Security

Terrorism

Utopias

Women in Politics

World

- General
- African
- Asian
- Australian & Oceanian
- Canadian
- Caribbean & Latin American
- European
- Middle Eastern
- Russian & Former Soviet Union

Psychology

General

Applied Psychology

Assessment, Testing & Measurement

Clinical Psychology

Cognitive Neuroscience & Cognitive Neuropsychology

Cognitive Psychology & Cognition

Creative Ability

Developmental

- General
- Adolescent
- Adulthood & Aging

- Child
- Lifespan Development

Education & Training

Emotions

Ethnopsychology

Experimental Psychology

Forensic Psychology

Grief & Loss

History

Human Sexuality

Hypnotism

Industrial & Organizational Psychology

Interpersonal Relations

Mental Health

Movements

- General
- Behaviorism
- Cognitive Behavioral Therapy
- Existential
- Gestalt
- Humanistic
- Jungian
- Psychoanalysis
- Transpersonal

Neuropsychology

Personality

Physiological Psychology

Practice Management

Psychopathology

- General
- Addiction
- Anxieties & Phobias
- Attention-Deficit Disorder
- Autism Spectrum Disorders
- Bipolar Disorder
- Compulsive Behavior

- Depression
- Dissociative Identity Disorder
- Eating Disorders
- Personality Disorders
- Post-Traumatic Stress Disorder
- Schizophrenia

Psychotherapy

- General
- Child & Adolescent
- Counseling
- Couples & Family
- Group
- Reference
- Research & Methodology
- Social Psychology
- Statistics
- Suicide

Religion / Religion & Spirituality

General
Agnosticism
Ancient
Antiquities & Archaeology
Atheism
Baha'i
Biblical Biography

- General
- New Testament
- Old Testament

Biblical Commentary

- General
- New Testament
- Old Testament

Biblical Criticism & Interpretation

- General

- New Testament
- Old Testament

Biblical Meditations
- General
- New Testament
- Old Testament

Biblical Reference
- General
- Atlases
- Concordances
- Dictionaries & Encyclopedias
- Handbooks
- Language Study
- Quotations

Biblical Studies
- General
- Bible Study Guides
- Exegesis & Hermeneutics
- History & Culture
- Jesus, the Gospels & Acts
- New Testament
- Old Testament
- Paul's Letters
- Prophecy
- Prophets
- Wisdom Literature

Blasphemy, Heresy & Apostasy
Buddhism
- General
- History
- Rituals & Practice
- Sacred Writings
- Theravada
- Tibetan
- Zen

Christian Church

- General
- Administration
- Canon & Ecclesiastical Law
- Growth
- History
- Leadership

Christian Education

- General
- Adult
- Children & Youth

Christian Life

- General
- Death, Grief, Bereavement
- Devotional
- Family
- Inspirational
- Love & Marriage
- Men's Issues
- Personal Growth
- Prayer
- Professional Growth
- Relationships
- Social Issues
- Spiritual Growth
- Spiritual Warfare
- Stewardship & Giving
- Women's Issues

Christian Ministry

- General
- Adult
- Children
- Counseling & Recovery
- Discipleship
- Evangelism
- Missions
- Pastoral Resources

- Preaching
- Youth

Christian Rituals & Practice
- General
- Sacraments
- Worship & Liturgy

Christian Theology
- General
- Angelology & Demonology
- Anthropology
- Apologetics
- Christology
- Ecclesiology
- Eschatology
- Ethics
- History
- Liberation
- Mariology
- Pneumatology
- Process
- Soteriology
- Systematic

Christianity
- General
- Amish
- Anglican
- Baptist
- Calvinist
- Catechisms
- Catholic
- Christian Science
- Church of Jesus Christ of Latter-day Saints
- Denominations
- Episcopalian
- History

- Jehovah's Witnesses
- Literature & the Arts
- Lutheran
- Mennonite
- Methodist
- Orthodox
- Pentecostal & Charismatic
- Presbyterian
- Protestant
- Quaker
- Saints & Sainthood
- Seventh-Day Adventist
- Shaker
- United Church of Christ

Clergy
Comparative Religion
Confucianism
Counseling
Cults
Deism
Demonology & Satanism
Devotional
Eastern
Eckankar
Ecumenism & Interfaith
Education
Eschatology
Essays
Ethics
Ethnic & Tribal
Faith
Fundamentalism
Gnosticism
Hinduism
- General
- History

- Rituals & Practice
- Sacred Writings
- Theology

History

Holidays

- General
- Christian
- Christmas & Advent
- Easter & Lent
- Jewish
- Other

Inspirational

Institutions & Organizations

Islam

- General
- History
- Koran & Sacred Writings
- Law
- Rituals & Practice
- Shi'a
- Sufi
- Sunni
- Theology

Jainism

Judaism

- General
- Conservative
- History
- Kabbalah & Mysticism
- Orthodox
- Reform
- Rituals & Practice
- Sacred Writings
- Talmud
- Theology

Leadership

Meditations
Messianic Judaism
Monasticism
Mysticism
Paganism & Neo-Paganism
Philosophy
Prayer
Prayerbooks
- General
- Christian
- Islamic
- Jewish

Psychology of Religion
Reference
Religion & Science
Religion, Politics & State
Religious Intolerance, Persecution & Conflict
Scientology
Sermons
- General
- Christian
- Jewish

Sexuality & Gender Studies
Shintoism
Sikhism
Spirituality
Taoism
Theism
Theology
Theosophy
Unitarian Universalism
Wicca
Zoroastrianism

Science

General
Acoustics & Sound
Applied Sciences
Astronomy
Biotechnology
Chaotic Behavior in Systems
Chemistry
- General
- Analytic
- Clinical
- Computational & Molecular Modeling
- Environmental
- Industrial & Technical
- Inorganic
- Organic
- Physical & Theoretical
- Toxicology

Cognitive Science
Cosmology
Earth Sciences
- General
- Geography
- Geology
- Hydrology
- Limnology
- Meteorology & Climatology
- Mineralogy
- Oceanography
- Sedimentology & Stratigraphy
- Seismology & Volcanism

Electron Microscopes & Microscopy
Energy
Environmental Science
Essays

Experiments & Projects
Global Warming & Climate Change
Gravity
History
Laboratory Techniques
Life Sciences

- General
- Anatomy & Physiology
- Bacteriology
- Biochemistry
- Biological Diversity
- Biology
- Biophysics
- Botany
- Cell Biology
- Developmental Biology
- Ecology
- Evolution
- Genetics & Genomics
- Horticulture
- Human Anatomy & Physiology
- Marine Biology
- Microbiology
- Molecular Biology
- Mycology
- Neuroscience
- Taxonomy
- Virology
- Zoology
    - General
    - Entomology
    - Ichthyology & Herpetology
    - Invertebrates
    - Mammals
    - Ornithology
    - Primatology

Mechanics
- General
- Aerodynamics
- Dynamics
- Fluids
- Hydrodynamics
- Solids
- Statics
- Thermodynamics

Microscopes & Microscopy
Nanoscience
Natural History
Paleontology
Philosophy & Social Aspects
Physics
- General
- Astrophysics
- Atomic & Molecular
- Condensed Matter
- Crystallography
- Electricity
- Electromagnetism
- Geophysics
- Magnetism
- Mathematical & Computational
- Nuclear
- Optics & Light
- Polymer
- Quantum Theory
- Relativity

Radiation
Radiology
Reference
Research & Methodology
Scientific Instruments
Space Science

Spectroscopy & Spectrum Analysis
Study & Teaching
System Theory
Time
Waves & Wave Mechanics
Weights & Measures

Self-Help

General
Abuse
Adult Children of Substance Abusers
Affirmations
Aging
Anger Management
Anxieties & Phobias
Codependency
Communication & Social Skills
Compulsive Behavior
- General
- Gambling
- Hoarding
- Obsessive Compulsive Disorder
- Sex & Pornography Addiction

Creativity
Death, Grief, Bereavement
Dreams
Eating Disorders & Body Image
Emotions
Fashion & Style
Green Lifestyle
Handwriting Analysis
Meditations
Mood Disorders
- General
- Bipolar Disorder

- Depression

Motivational & Inspirational

Neuro-Linguistic Programming

Personal Growth

- General
- Happiness
- Memory Improvement
- Self-Esteem
- Success

Post-Traumatic Stress Disorder (PTSD)

Self-Hypnosis

Self-Management

- General
- Stress Management
- Time Management

Sexual Instruction

Spiritual

Substance Abuse & Addictions

- General
- Alcohol
- Drugs
- Tobacco

Twelve-Step Programs

Social Sciences

General

Abortion & Birth Control

Agriculture & Food

Anthropology

- General
- Cultural
- Physical

Archaeology

Black Studies

Body Language & Nonverbal Communication

Children's Studies
Conspiracy Theories
Criminology
Customs & Traditions
Death & Dying
Demography
Developing & Emerging Countries
Disasters & Disaster Relief
Discrimination & Race Relations
Disease & Health Issues
Emigration & Immigration
Essays
Ethnic Studies
- General
- African American Studies
- Asian American Studies
- Hispanic American Studies
- Native American Studies
Feminism & Feminist Theory
Folklore & Mythology
Freemasonry & Secret Societies
Future Studies
Gay Studies
Gender Studies
Gerontology
Holidays
Human Geography
Human Services
Indigenous Studies
Islamic Studies
Jewish Studies
Lesbian Studies
Media Studies
Men's Studies
Methodology
Minority Studies

Penology
People with Disabilities
Philanthropy & Charity
Popular Culture
Pornography
Poverty & Homelessness
Prostitution & Sex Trade
Reference
Regional Studies
Research
Sexual Abuse & Harassment
Slavery
Social Classes
Social Work
Sociology
- General
- Marriage & Family
- Rural
- Urban

Sociology of Religion
Statistics
Violence in Society
Volunteer Work
Women's Studies

Sports & Recreation

General
Air Sports
Archery
Baseball
- General
- Essays & Writings
- History
- Statistics

Basketball

Boating

Bodybuilding & Weight Training

Bowling

Boxing

Business Aspects

Camping

Canoeing

Caving

Cheerleading

Coaching

- General
- Baseball
- Basketball
- Football
- Soccer

Cricket

Cycling

Dog Racing

Equestrian

Equipment & Supplies

Essays

Extreme Sports

Fencing

Field Hockey

Fishing

Football

Golf

Gymnastics

Health & Safety

Hiking

History

Hockey

Horse Racing

Hunting

Ice & Figure Skating

Juggling

Kayaking
Lacrosse
Martial Arts & Self-Defense
Motor Sports
Mountaineering
Olympics
Outdoor Skills
Polo
Pool, Billiards, Snooker
Racket Sports
Racquetball
Reference
Rodeos
Roller & In-Line Skating
Rugby
Running & Jogging
Sailing
Scuba & Snorkeling
Shooting
Skateboarding
Skiing
Snowboarding
Soccer
Sociology of Sports
Softball
Sports Psychology
Squash
Surfing
Swimming & Diving
Table Tennis
Tennis
Track & Field
Training
Triathlon
Volleyball
Walking

Water Sports
Winter Sports
Wrestling

Technology & Engineering

General
Acoustics & Sound
Aeronautics & Astronautics
Agriculture
- General
- Agronomy
  - General
  - Crop Science
  - Soil Science
- Animal Husbandry
- Beekeeping
- Enology & Viticulture
- Forestry
- Irrigation
- Organic
- Sustainable Agriculture
- Tropical Agriculture

Automation
Automotive
Biomedical
Cartography
Chemical & Biochemical
Civil
- General
- Bridges
- Dams & Reservoirs
- Earthquake
- Flood Control
- Highway & Traffic
- Soil & Rock

- Transport

Construction
- General
- Carpentry
- Contracting
- Electrical
- Estimating
- Heating, Ventilation & Air Conditioning
- Masonry
- Plumbing
- Roofing

Drafting & Mechanical Drawing

Electrical

Electronics
- General
- Circuits
  - General
  - Integrated
  - Logic
  - VLSI & ULSI
- Digital
- Microelectronics
- Optoelectronics
- Semiconductors
- Solid State
- Transistors

Emergency Management

Engineering

Environmental
- General
- Pollution Control
- Waste Management
- Water Supply

Fiber Optics

Fire Science

Fisheries & Aquaculture

Food Science
Fracture Mechanics
History
Holography
Hydraulics
Imaging Systems
Industrial Design
- General
- Packaging
- Product

Industrial Engineering
Industrial Health & Safety
Industrial Technology
Inventions
Lasers & Photonics
Machinery
Manufacturing
Marine & Naval
Materials Science
Measurement
Mechanical
Metallurgy
Microwaves
Military Science
Mining
Mobile & Wireless Communications
Nanotechnology & MEMS
Operations Research
Optics
Pest Control
Petroleum
Power Resources
- General
- Alternative & Renewable
- Electrical
- Fossil Fuels

- Nuclear

Project Management

Quality Control

Radar

Radio

Reference

Remote Sensing & Geographic Information Systems

Research

Robotics

Sensors

Signals & Signal Processing

Social Aspects

Structural

Superconductors & Superconductivity

Surveying

Technical & Manufacturing Industries & Trades

Technical Writing

Telecommunications

Television & Video

Textiles & Polymers

Tribology

Transportation

General

Automotive

- General
- Antique & Classic
- Buyer's Guides
- Customizing
- History
- Pictorial
- Repair & Maintenance
- Trucks

Aviation

- General

- Commercial
- History
- Piloting & Flight Instruction
- Repair & Maintenance

Bicycles

Motorcycles
- General
- History
- Pictorial
- Repair & Maintenance

Navigation

Public Transportation

Railroads
- General
- History
- Pictorial

Ships & Shipbuilding
- General
- History
- Pictorial
- Repair & Maintenance

Travel

General

Africa
- General
- Central
- East
- Kenya
- Morocco
- North
- Republic of South Africa
- South
- West

Amusement & Theme Parks

AMAZON CATEGORIES

Asia
- General
- Central
- China
- Far East
- India & South Asia
- Japan
- Southeast
- Southwest

Australia & Oceania

Bed & Breakfast

Budget

Canada
- General
- Atlantic Provinces
- Ontario
- Prairie Provinces
- Quebec
- Territories & Nunavut
- Western Provinces

Caribbean & West Indies

Central America

Cruises

Essays & Travelogues

Europe
- General
- Austria
- Benelux Countries
- Cyprus
- Denmark
- Eastern
- France
- Germany
- Great Britain
- Greece
- Iceland & Greenland

- Ireland
- Italy
- Scandinavia
- Spain & Portugal
- Switzerland
- Western

Former Soviet Republics

Hikes & Walks

Hotels, Inns & Hostels

Maps & Road Atlases

Mexico

Middle East

- General
- Egypt
- Israel
- Turkey

Museums, Tours, Points of Interest

Parks & Campgrounds

Pictorials

Polar Regions

Rail Travel

Reference

Resorts & Spas

Restaurants

Road Travel

Russia

Shopping

South America

- General
- Argentina
- Brazil
- Chile & Easter Island
- Ecuador & Galapagos Islands
- Peru

Special Interest

- General

- Adventure
- Business
- Disabilities & Special Needs
- Ecotourism
- Family
- LGBT
- Literary
- Pets
- Religious
- Senior
- Sports

United States

- General
- Midwest
    - General
    - East North Central
    - West North Central
- Northeast
    - General
    - Middle Atlantic
    - New England
- South
    - General
    - East South Central
    - South Atlantic
    - West South Central
- West
    - General
    - Mountain
    - Pacific

True Crime

General
Espionage
Hoaxes & Deceptions

Murder
- General
- Serial Killers

Organized Crime

White Collar Crime

JUVENILE FICTION

Juvenile Fiction

General

Action & Adventure
- General
- Pirates
- Survival Stories

Activity Books

Animals
- General
- Alligators & Crocodiles
- Apes, Monkeys, etc.
- Baby Animals
- Bears
- Birds
- Butterflies, Moths & Caterpillars
- Cats
- Cows
- Deer, Moose & Caribou
- Dinosaurs & Prehistoric Creatures
- Dogs
- Dragons, Unicorns & Mythical
- Ducks, Geese, etc.
- Elephants
- Farm Animals
- Fishes
- Foxes
- Frogs & Toads

AMAZON CATEGORIES

- Giraffes
- Hippos & Rhinos
- Horses
- Insects, Spiders, etc.
- Jungle Animals
- Kangaroos
- Lions, Tigers, Leopards, etc.
- Mammals
- Marine Life
- Mice, Hamsters, Guinea Pigs, etc.
- Nocturnal
- Pets
- Pigs
- Rabbits
- Reptiles & Amphibians
- Squirrels
- Turtles
- Wolves & Coyotes
- Zoos

Art & Architecture
Bedtime & Dreams
Biographical
- General
- Canada
- European
- Other
- United States

Books & Libraries
Boys & Men
Business, Careers, Occupations
Classics
Clothing & Dress
Comics & Graphic Novels
- General
- Manga
- Media Tie-In

- Superheroes

Computers

Concepts

- General
- Alphabet
- Body
- Colors
- Counting & Numbers
- Date & Time
- Money
- Opposites
- Seasons
- Senses & Sensation
- Size & Shape
- Sounds
- Words

Cooking & Food

Dystopian

Fairy Tales & Folklore

- General
- Adaptations
- Anthologies
- Country & Ethnic

Family

- General
- Adoption
- Alternative Family
- Marriage & Divorce
- Multigenerational
- New Baby
- Orphans & Foster Homes
- Parents
- Siblings
- Stepfamilies

Fantasy & Magic

Girls & Women

AMAZON CATEGORIES

Health & Daily Living
- General
- Daily Activities
- Diseases, Illnesses & Injuries
- Toilet Training

Historical
- General
- Africa
- Ancient Civilizations
- Asia
- Canada
    - General
    - Post-Confederation
    - Pre-Confederation
- Europe
- Exploration & Discovery
- Holocaust
- Medieval
- Middle East
- Military & Wars
- Other
- Prehistory
- Renaissance
- United States
    - General
    - 19th Century
    - 20th Century
    - 21st Century
    - Civil War Period
    - Colonial & Revolutionary Periods

Holidays & Celebrations
- General
- Birthdays
- Christmas & Advent
- Easter & Lent
- Halloween

- Hanukkah
- Kwanzaa
- Other, Non-Religious
- Other, Religious
- Passover
- Patriotic Holidays
- Thanksgiving
- Valentine's Day

Horror & Ghost Stories
Humorous Stories
Imagination & Play
Interactive Adventures
Law & Crime
Legends, Myths, Fables

- General
- Arthurian
- Greek & Roman
- Norse
- Other

LGBT
Lifestyles

- City & Town Life
- Country Life
- Farm & Ranch Life

Love & Romance
Media Tie-In
Monsters
Mysteries & Detective Stories
Nature & the Natural World

- General
- Environment
- Weather

Nursery Rhymes
Paranormal
People & Places

- General

- Africa
- Asia
- Australia & Oceania
- Canada
  - General
  - Native Canadian
- Caribbean & Latin America
- Europe
- Mexico
- Middle East
- Other
- Polar Regions
- United States
  - General
  - African American
  - Asian American
  - Hispanic & Latino
  - Native American
  - Other

Performing Arts
- General
- Circus
- Dance
- Film
- Music
- Television & Radio
- Theater

Picture Books

Politics & Government

Readers
- Beginner
- Chapter Books
- Intermediate

Recycling & Green Living

Religious
- General

- Christian
  - General
  - Action & Adventure
  - Animals
  - Bedtime & Dreams
  - Comics & Graphic Novels
  - Early Readers
  - Emotions & Feelings
  - Family
  - Fantasy
  - Friendship
  - Historical
  - Holidays & Celebrations
  - Humorous
  - Learning Concepts
  - Mysteries & Detective Stories
  - People & Places
  - Relationships
  - Science Fiction
  - Social Issues
  - Sports & Recreation
  - Values & Virtues
- Jewish
- Other

Robots
Royalty
School & Education
Science & Technology
Science Fiction
Short Stories
Social Issues
- General
- Adolescence
- Bullying
- Dating & Sex
- Death & Dying

- Depression & Mental Illness
- Drugs, Alcohol, Substance Abuse
- Emigration & Immigration
- Emotions & Feelings
- Friendship
- Homelessness & Poverty
- Homosexuality
- Manners & Etiquette
- New Experience
- Peer Pressure
- Physical & Emotional Abuse
- Pregnancy
- Prejudice & Racism
- Runaways
- Self-Esteem & Self-Reliance
- Self-Mutilation
- Sexual Abuse
- Special Needs
- Strangers
- Suicide
- Values & Virtues
- Violence

Sports & Recreation
- General
- Baseball & Softball
- Basketball
- Camping & Outdoor Activities
- Cycling
- Equestrian
- Extreme Sports
- Football
- Games
- Golf
- Hockey
- Ice Skating
- Martial Arts

- Miscellaneous
- Roller & In-Line Skating
- Skateboarding
- Soccer
- Water Sports
- Winter Sports
- Wrestling

Steampunk

Stories in Verse

Time Travel

Toys, Dolls & Puppets

Transportation

- General
- Aviation
- Boats, Ships & Underwater Craft
- Cars & Trucks
- Motorcycles
- Railroads & Trains

Visionary & Metaphysical

Westerns

JUVENILE NON-FICTION

Juveline Non-Fiction

General

Activity Books

Adventure & Adventurers

Animals

- General
- Animal Welfare
- Apes, Monkeys, etc.
- Baby Animals
- Bears
- Birds
- Butterflies, Moths & Caterpillars

- Cats
- Cows
- Deer, Moose & Caribou
- Dinosaurs & Prehistoric Creatures
- Dogs
- Ducks, Geese, etc.
- Elephants
- Endangered
- Farm Animals
- Fishes
- Foxes
- Giraffes
- Hippos & Rhinos
- Horses
- Insects, Spiders, etc.
- Jungle Animals
- Kangaroos
- Lions, Tigers, Leopards, etc.
- Mammals
- Marine Life
- Mice, Hamsters, Guinea Pigs, Squirrels, etc.
- Nocturnal
- Pets
- Rabbits
- Reptiles & Amphibians
- Wolves & Coyotes
- Zoos

Antiques & Collectibles
Architecture
Art

- General
- Cartooning
- Drawing
- Fashion
- History
- Painting

- Sculpture
- Techniques

Biography & Autobiography
- General
- Art
- Cultural Heritage
- Historical
- Literary
- Music
- Performing Arts
- Political
- Presidents & First Families
- Religious
- Royalty
- Science & Technology
- Social Activists
- Sports & Recreation
- Women

Body, Mind & Spirit

Books & Libraries

Boys & Men

Business & Economics

Careers

Clothing & Dress

Comics & Graphic Novels
- General
- Biography
- History

Computers
- General
- Entertainment & Games
- Internet
- Programming
- Software

Concepts
- General

AMAZON CATEGORIES

- Alphabet
- Body
- Colors
- Counting & Numbers
- Date & Time
- Money
- Opposites
- Seasons
- Senses & Sensation
- Size & Shape
- Sounds

Cooking & Food
Crafts & Hobbies
Curiosities & Wonders
Drama
Family
- General
- Adoption
- Alternative Family
- Marriage & Divorce
- Multigenerational
- New Baby
- Orphans & Foster Homes
- Parents
- Siblings
- Stepfamilies

Foreign Language Study
- General
- English as a Second Language
- French
- Spanish

Games & Activities
- General
- Board Games
- Card Games
- Magic

- Puzzles
- Questions & Answers
- Video & Electronic Games
- Word Games

Gardening

Girls & Women

Health & Daily Living

- General
- Daily Activities
- Diet & Nutrition
- Diseases, Illnesses & Injuries
- First Aid
- Fitness & Exercise
- Maturing
- Personal Hygiene
- Physical Impairments
- Safety
- Sexuality & Pregnancy
- Substance Abuse
- Toilet Training

History

- General
- Africa
- Ancient
- Asia
- Australia & Oceania
- Canada
  - General
  - Post-Confederation
  - Pre-Confederation
- Central & South America
- Europe
- Exploration & Discovery
- Holocaust
- Medieval
- Mexico

- Middle East
- Military & Wars
- Modern
- Other
- Prehistoric
- Renaissance
- Symbols, Monuments, National Parks, etc.
- United States
  - General
  - 19th Century
  - 20th Century
  - 21st Century
  - Civil War Period
  - Colonial & Revolutionary Periods
  - State & Local

Holidays & Celebrations
- General
- Birthdays
- Christmas & Advent
- Easter & Lent
- Halloween
- Hanukkah
- Kwanzaa
- Other, Non-Religious
- Other, Religious
- Passover
- Patriotic Holidays
- Thanksgiving
- Valentine's Day

House & Home

Humor
- General
- Comic Strips & Cartoons
- Jokes & Riddles

Language Arts
- General

- Composition & Creative Writing
- Grammar
- Handwriting
- Journal Writing
- Sign Language
- Vocabulary & Spelling

Law & Crime

Lifestyles

- City & Town Life
- Country Life
- Farm & Ranch Life

Literary Criticism & Collections

Mathematics

- General
- Advanced
- Algebra
- Arithmetic
- Fractions
- Geometry

Media Studies

Media Tie-In

Music

- General
- Classical
- History
- Instruction & Study
- Instruments
- Jazz
- Popular
- Rap & Hip Hop
- Rock
- Songbooks

People & Places

- General
- Africa
- Asia

- Australia & Oceania
- Canada
  - General
  - Native Canadian
- Caribbean & Latin America
- Europe
- Mexico
- Middle East
- Other
- Polar Regions
- United States
  - General
  - African American
  - Asian American
  - Hispanic & Latino
  - Native American
  - Other

Performing Arts
- General
- Circus
- Dance
- Film
- Television & Radio
- Theater

Philosophy

Photography

Poetry
- General
- Humorous

Readers
- Beginner
- Chapter Books
- Intermediate

Recycling & Green Living

Reference
- General

- Almanacs
- Atlases
- Dictionaries
- Encyclopedias
- Thesauri

Religion
- Stories General
- Bible
    - General
    - New Testament
    - Old Testament
- Biblical Biography
- Biblical Commentaries & Interpretation
- Biblical Reference
- Biblical Studies
- Christianity
- Eastern
- Islam
- Judaism

Religious
- Christian

School & Education

Science & Nature
- General
- Anatomy & Physiology
- Astronomy
- Biology
- Botany
- Chemistry
- Disasters
- Discoveries
- Earth Sciences
    - General
    - Earthquakes & Volcanoes
    - Geography
    - Rocks & Minerals

- Water
  - Weather
- Environmental Conservation & Protection
- Environmental Science & Ecosystems
- Experiments & Projects
- Flowers & Plants
- Fossils
- History of Science
- Physics
- Trees & Forests
- Weights & Measures
- Zoology

Social Issues
- General
- Adolescence
- Bullying
- Dating & Sex
- Death & Dying
- Depression & Mental Illness
- Drugs, Alcohol, Substance Abuse
- Emigration & Immigration
- Emotions & Feelings
- Friendship
- Homelessness & Poverty
- Homosexuality
- Manners & Etiquette
- New Experience
- Peer Pressure
- Physical & Emotional Abuse
- Pregnancy
- Prejudice & Racism
- Runaways
- Self-Esteem & Self-Reliance
- Self-Mutilation
- Sexual Abuse
- Special Needs

- Strangers
- Suicide
- Values & Virtues
- Violence

Social Science

- General
- Archaeology
- Customs, Traditions, Anthropology
- Folklore & Mythology
- Politics & Government
- Psychology
- Sociology

Sports & Recreation

- General
- Baseball & Softball
- Basketball
- Camping & Outdoor Activities
- Cycling
- Equestrian
- Extreme Sports
- Football
- Golf
- Gymnastics
- Hockey
- Ice Skating
- Martial Arts
- Miscellaneous
- Motor Sports
- Olympics
- Racket Sports
- Roller & In-Line Skating
- Skateboarding
- Soccer
- Track & Field
- Water Sports
- Winter Sports

- Wrestling

Study Aids
- General
- Book Notes
- Test Preparation

Technology
- General
- Aeronautics, Astronautics & Space Science
- Agriculture
- Electricity & Electronics
- How Things Work-Are Made
- Inventions
- Machinery & Tools

Toys, Dolls & Puppets

Transportation
- General
- Aviation
- Boats, Ships & Underwater Craft
- Cars & Trucks
- Motorcycles
- Railroads & Trains

Travel

COMICS & GRAPHIC NOVELS

Comics & Graphic Novels

General
Adaptations
Anthologies
Contemporary Women
Crime & Mystery
Erotica
Fantasy
Historical Fiction

Horror

LGBT

Literary

Manga

- General
- Adult Comics
- Boys' Love Comics
- Crime & Mystery
- Erotica
- Fantasy
- Historical Fiction
- Horror
- Illustrations & Fanbooks
- Josei Manga
- LGBT
- Media Tie-In
- Nonfiction
- Romance
- Science Fiction
- Seinen Manga
- Shonen Manga
- Shoujo Manga
- Sports
- Yaoi Manga

Media Tie-In

Nonfiction

Religious

Romance

Science Fiction

Superheroes

EDUCATORS & REFERENCE

Education

General

Administration
- General
- Elementary & Secondary
- Facility Management
- Higher
- School Superintendents & Principals

Adult & Continuing Education

Aims & Objectives

Arts in Education

Behavioral Management

Bilingual Education

Classroom Management

Collaborative & Team Teaching

Comparative

Computers & Technology

Counseling
- General
- Academic Development
- Career Development
- Crisis Management

Curricula

Decision-Making & Problem Solving

Distance & Online Education

Driver Education

Educational Policy & Reform
- General
- Charter Schools
- Federal Legislation
- School Safety

Educational Psychology

Elementary

Essays

Evaluation & Assessment

Experimental Methods

Finance

Higher

History
Home Schooling
Inclusive Education
Language Experience Approach
Leadership
Learning Styles
Multicultural Education
Non-Formal Education
Organizations & Institutions
Parent Participation
Philosophy & Social Aspects
Physical Education
Preschool & Kindergarten
Professional Development
Reference
Research
Rural
Secondary
Special Education
- General
- Communicative Disorders
- Gifted
- Learning Disabilities
- Mental Disabilities
- Physical Disabilities
- Social Disabilities

Statistics
Student Life & Student Affairs
Study Skills
Teaching Methods & Materials
- General
- Arts & Humanities
- Health & Sexuality
- Language Arts
- Library Skills
- Mathematics

- Reading & Phonics
- Science & Technology
- Social Science

Testing & Measurement
Training & Certification
Urban
Violence & Harassment
Vocational

Foreign Language Study

General
African Languages
Ancient Languages
Arabic
Baltic Languages
Celtic Languages
Chinese
Creole Languages
Czech
Danish
Dutch
English as a Second Language
Finnish
French
German
Greek
Hebrew
Hindi
Hungarian
Indic Languages
Italian
Japanese
Korean
Latin
Miscellaneous

Multi-Language Dictionaries
Multi-Language Phrasebooks
Native American Languages
Norwegian
Oceanic & Australian Languages
Old & Middle English
Persian
Polish
Portuguese
Romance Languages
Russian
Scandinavian Languages
Serbian & Croatian
Slavic Languages
Southeast Asian Languages
Spanish
Swahili
Swedish
Turkish & Turkic Languages
Vietnamese
Yiddish

Reference

General
Almanacs
Atlases, Gazetteers & Maps
Bibliographies & Indexes
Catalogs
Consumer Guides
Curiosities & Wonders
Dictionaries
Directories
Encyclopedias
Etiquette
Genealogy & Heraldry

Handbooks & Manuals
Japanese Non Fiction
Personal & Practical Guides
Questions & Answers
Quotations
Research
Survival & Emergency Preparedness
Thesauri
Trivia
Weddings
Word Lists
Writing Skills
Yearbooks & Annuals

Study Aids

General
ACT
Advanced Placement
Armed Forces
Bar Exam
Book Notes
Citizenship
Civil Service
CLEP
College Entrance
College Guides
CPA
Financial Aid
GED
GMAT
Graduate School Guides
GRE
High School Entrance
LSAT
MAT

MCAT
NTE
Professional
PSAT & NMSQT
Regents
SAT
Study Guides
Tests
TOEFL
Vocational

LITERARY COLLECTIONS

Literary Collections

General
African
American

- General
- African American

Ancient & Classical
Asian

- General
- Chinese
- Indic
- Japanese

Australian & Oceanian
Canadian
Caribbean & Latin American
Diaries & Journals
Essays
European

- General
- Eastern
- English, Irish, Scottish, Welsh
- French

- German
- Italian
- Scandinavian
- Spanish & Portuguese

Letters
LGBT
Medieval
Middle Eastern
Native American
Russian & Former Soviet Union
Speeches
Women Authors

NON-CLASSIFIABLE

EXAMPLES OF AMAZON CATEGORIES THAT REQUIRE SPECIFIC KEYWORDS

In order to ensure that Amazon places your books in the correct category, please check their KEYWORD REQUREMENTS - https://kdp.amazon.com/help?topicId=A200PDGPEIQX41

BIOGRAPHIES & MEMOIRS
- Biographies & Memoirs/Leaders & Notable People/Religious/Christianity – *christian, christianity*

BUSINESS & MONEY
- Business & Money/Entrepreneurship & Small Business/Startups – *startup, startups*
- Business & Money/Biographies & Primers/Inspiration – *inspiration, inspirational*
- Business & Money/Business Life/Health & Stress – *health, stress*
- Business & Money/Personal Finance/Financial Planning – *financial planning*
- Business & Money/Entrepreneurship & Small Business/Legal Guides – *legal guides*

CHILDREN'S EBOOKS
- Children's Age Range/ Baby-2 – *baby*
- Children's Age Range/ Ages 3-5 – *preschool*
- Children's Age Range/ Ages 6-8 – *ages 6-8*
- Children's Age Range/ 9-12 – *preteen*
- Children's Fantasy & Magic/Coming of Age – *coming of age*

- Children's Fantasy & Magic/Sword & Sorcery – *sword, sorcery, magic, dragon, quest*
- Children's Mystery & Thrillers/Detectives – *detective, sleuth*
- Children's Mystery & Thrillers/Fantasy & Supernatural – *fantasy, paranormal, magic*
- Children's Mystery & Thrillers/Spies – *spy, terrorist, secret agent*
- Children's Science Fiction/Action & Adventure – *action, adventure*
- Children's Science Fiction/Action & Adventure/Superheroes – superhero
- Children's Science Fiction/Aliens – *alien, extraterrestrial*
- Children's Science Fiction/Time Travel – *time travel*

HEALTH, FITNESS & DIETING

- Health, Fitness & Dieting/Counseling & Psychology/Developmental Psychology/Adulthood &   Aging – *adult, developmental psychology*
- Health, Fitness & Dieting/Counseling & Psychology/Developmental Psychology/Lifespan Development – *lifespan development*
- Health, Fitness & Dieting/Counseling & Psychology/Grief & Loss – *grief*
- Health, Fitness & Dieting/Diseases & Physical Ailments/Alzheimer's Disease – *alzheimer*

RELIGION & SPIRITUALITY

- Religion & Spirituality/Christian Books & Bibles/Bibles/More Translations/Evangelical – *evangelical*
- Religion & Spirituality/Christian Books & Bibles/Bibles/More Translations/Life Application – *life application*
- Religion & Spirituality/Christian Books & Bibles/Bibles/More Translations/Spanish Language – *spanish*
- Religion & Spirituality/Christian Books & Bibles/Christian Fiction/Poetry – *christian poetry*
- Religion & Spirituality/Christian Books & Bibles/Christian Living/Counseling – *christian, christianity*

- Religion & Spirituality/Christian Books & Bibles/Christian Living/Music/Hymns – *christian, christians, christianity*
- Religion & Spirituality/Christian Books & Bibles/Christian Living/Self-Help – *self-help, self help*
- Religion & Spirituality/Christian Books & Bibles/History/Historical Jesus – *historical jesus*
- Religion & Spirituality/Christian Books & Bibles/Protestantism/Inspirational – *inspire, inspires, inspiration, inspirational*
- Religion & Spirituality/Christian Books & Bibles/Protestantism/Self-Help – *self-help, self help*
- Religion & Spirituality/Christian Books & Bibles/Theology/Creationism – *creationism*
- Religion & Spirituality/Christian Books & Bibles/Theology/Prophecy – *prophecy*
- Religion & Spirituality/Christian Books & Bibles/Worship & Devotion/Meditations – *meditation, meditations, meditating*
- Religion & Spirituality/Islam/Muhammad – *muhammad, muhammed, mohammed*
- Religion & Spirituality/Judaism/Sacred Writings/Hebrew Bible (Old Testament)/Hebrew – *hebrew*
- Religion & Spirituality/Occult/Ghosts & Haunted Houses/Ghosts – *ghost, ghosts*
- Religion & Spirituality/Occult/Ghosts & Haunted Houses/Haunted Houses – *haunted house, haunted houses*
- Religion & Spirituality/Spirituality/Gifts – *spiritual gift, spiritual gifts*
- Religion & Spirituality/Spirituality/Inspirational/Conduct of Life – *conduct of life*
- Religion & Spirituality/Spirituality/Inspirational/Death & Grief – *death, dying, grief, bereavement*
- Religion & Spirituality/Spirituality/Inspirational/Family – *family*
- Religion & Spirituality/Spirituality/Inspirational/Health – *health, healthy, sickness, sick, illness*
- Religion & Spirituality/Spirituality/Inspirational/Men's Inspirational – *man, men*

- Religion & Spirituality/Spirituality/Inspirational/Miracles –*miracle, miracles*
- Religion & Spirituality/Spirituality/Inspirational/Personal Testimonies – *personal testimony, personal testimonies*
- Religion & Spirituality/Spirituality/Inspirational/Relationships – *relationship, relationships, dating*
- Religion & Spirituality/Spirituality/Inspirational/Women's Inspirational – *woman, women*
- Religion & Spirituality/Spirituality/Personal Growth/Family – *family*
- Religion & Spirituality/Spirituality/Personal Growth/Men's Personal Growth – *man, men*
- Religion & Spirituality/Spirituality/Personal Growth/Motivational – *motivation, motivational*
- Religion & Spirituality/Spirituality/Personal Growth/Personal Success – *personal success*
- Religion & Spirituality/Spirituality/Personal Growth/Philosophy – *philosophy, philosophical*
- Religion & Spirituality/Spirituality/Personal Growth/Self-Help – *self-help, self help*
- Religion & Spirituality/Spirituality/Personal Growth/Spiritual Healing – *healing*
- Religion & Spirituality/Spirituality/Personal Growth/Transformational – *transformation, transformations, transformational*
- Religion & Spirituality/Spirituality/Personal Growth/Women's Personal Growth – *woman, women*
- Religion & Spirituality/Spirituality/Women – *woman, women*

BISAC CATEGORIES FOR USE PUBLISHING PRINT BOOKS ON AMAZON WITH CREATESPACE

ANTIQUES & COLLECTIBLES

ARCHITECTURE

ART

BIBLES

BIOGRAPHY & AUTOBIOGRAPHY

BODY, MIND & SPIRIT

- OCC000000 BODY, MIND & SPIRIT / General
- OCC022000 BODY, MIND & SPIRIT / Afterlife & Reincarnation
- OCC006000 BODY, MIND & SPIRIT / Dream
- OCC011000 BODY, MIND & SPIRIT / Healing / General
- OCC011020 BODY, MIND & SPIRIT / Healing / Prayer & Spiritual
- OCC019000 BODY, MIND & SPIRIT / Inspiration & Personal Growth
- OCC010000 BODY, MIND & SPIRIT / Mindfulness & Meditation
- OCC016000 BODY, MIND & SPIRIT / Occultism
- OCC034000 BODY, MIND & SPIRIT / Parapsychology / Near-Death Experience
- OCC020000 BODY, MIND & SPIRIT / Prophecy
- OCC021000 BODY, MIND & SPIRIT / Reference
- OCC027000 BODY, MIND & SPIRIT / Spiritualism

BUSINESS & ECONOMICS

- US000000 BUSINESS & ECONOMICS / General
- BUS002000 BUSINESS & ECONOMICS / Advertising & Promotion
- BUS006000 BUSINESS & ECONOMICS / Budgeting
- BUS090010 BUSINESS & ECONOMICS / E-Commerce / Internet Marketin

- BUS080000 BUSINESS & ECONOMICS / Home-Based Businesses
- BUSINESS & ECONOMICS / Hospitality, Travel & Tourism see Industries / Hospitality, Travel & Tourism

S081000 BUSINESS & ECONOMICS / Industries / Hospitality, Travel & Tourism

BUS106000 BUSINESS & ECONOMICS / Mentoring & Coaching

BUS046000 BUSINESS & ECONOMICS / Motivational

BUS107000 BUSINESS & ECONOMICS / Personal Success

COMICS & GRAPHIC NOVELS

COMPUTERS

COOKING

CRAFTS & HOBBIES

DESIGN

DRAMA

EDUCATION

FAMILY & RELATIONSHIPS

FICTION

FOREIGN LANGUAGE STUDY

GAMES

GARDENING

HEALTH & FITNESS

HISTORY

HOUSE & HOME

HUMOR

JUVENILE FICTION

JUVENILE NONFICTION

LANGUAGE ARTS & DISCIPLINES

LAW

LITERARY COLLECTIONS

AMAZON CATEGORIES

LITERARY CRITICISM

MATHEMATICS

MEDICAL

MUSIC

NATURE

PERFORMING ARTS

PETS

PHILOSOPHY

PHOTOGRAPHY

POETRY

POLITICAL SCIENCE

PSYCHOLOGY

REFERENCE

RELIGION

- REL000000 RELIGION / General
- REL001000 RELIGION / Agnosticism
- REL114000 RELIGION / Ancient
- REL072000 RELIGION / Antiquities & Archaeology
- RELIGION / Archaeology see Antiquities & Archaeology
- REL004000 RELIGION / Atheism
- REL005000 RELIGION / Baha'i
- REL006020 RELIGION / Biblical Biography / General
- REL006030 RELIGION / Biblical Biography / Old Testament
- REL006040 RELIGION / Biblical Biography / New Testament
- REL006050 RELIGION / Biblical Commentary / General
- REL006060 RELIGION / Biblical Commentary / Old Testament
- REL006070 RELIGION / Biblical Commentary / New Testament
- REL006080 RELIGION / Biblical Criticism & Interpretation / General
- REL006090 RELIGION / Biblical Criticism & Interpretation / Old Testament

- REL006100 RELIGION / Biblical Criticism & Interpretation / New Testament
- REL006110 RELIGION / Biblical Meditations / General
- REL006120 RELIGION / Biblical Meditations / Old Testament
- REL006130 RELIGION / Biblical Meditations / New Testament
- REL006160 RELIGION / Biblical Reference / General
- REL006650 RELIGION / Biblical Reference / Atlases
- REL006660 RELIGION / Biblical Reference / Concordances
- REL006670 RELIGION / Biblical Reference / Dictionaries & Encyclopedias
- REL006680 RELIGION / Biblical Reference / Handbooks
- REL006410 RELIGION / Biblical Reference / Language Study
- REL006150 RELIGION / Biblical Reference / Quotations
- REL006000 RELIGION / Biblical Studies / General
- REL006700 RELIGION / Biblical Studies / Bible Study Guides
- REL006400 RELIGION / Biblical Studies / Exegesis & Hermeneutics
- REL006630 RELIGION / Biblical Studies / History & Culture
- REL006710 RELIGION / Biblical Studies / Jesus, the Gospels & Acts
- REL006210 RELIGION / Biblical Studies / Old Testament
- REL006220 RELIGION / Biblical Studies / New Testament
- REL006720 RELIGION / Biblical Studies / Paul's Letters
- REL006140 RELIGION / Biblical Studies / Prophecy
- REL006730 RELIGION / Biblical Studies / Prophets
- REL006740 RELIGION / Biblical Studies / Wisdom Literature
- REL115000 RELIGION / Blasphemy, Heresy & Apostasy
- REL007000 RELIGION / Buddhism / General (see also PHILOSOPHY / Buddhist)
- REL007010 RELIGION / Buddhism / History
- REL007020 RELIGION / Buddhism / Rituals & Practice
- REL007030 RELIGION / Buddhism / Sacred Writings
- REL007040 RELIGION / Buddhism / Theravada
- REL007050 RELIGION / Buddhism / Tibetan
- REL092000 RELIGION / Buddhism / Zen (see also PHILOSOPHY / Zen)

AMAZON CATEGORIES

- RELIGION / Canon & Ecclesiastical Law see Christian Church / Canon & Ecclesiastical Law
- RELIGION / Catechisms see Christianity / Catechisms or specific non-Christian religions
- REL108000 RELIGION / Christian Church / General
- REL014000 RELIGION / Christian Church / Administration
- REL008000 RELIGION / Christian Church / Canon & Ecclesiastical Law
- REL108010 RELIGION / Christian Church / Growth
- REL108020 RELIGION / Christian Church / History
- REL108030 RELIGION / Christian Church / Leadership
- REL011000 RELIGION / Christian Education / General
- REL095000 RELIGION / Christian Education / Adult
- REL091000 RELIGION / Christian Education / Children & Youth
- REL012000 RELIGION / Christian Life / General
- REL012010 RELIGION / Christian Life / Death, Grief, Bereavement
- REL012020 RELIGION / Christian Life / Devotional
- REL012030 RELIGION / Christian Life / Family
- REL012040 RELIGION / Christian Life / Inspirational
- REL012050 RELIGION / Christian Life / Love & Marriage
- REL012060 RELIGION / Christian Life / Men's Issues
- REL012070 RELIGION / Christian Life / Personal Growth
- REL012080 RELIGION / Christian Life / Prayer
- REL012090 RELIGION / Christian Life / Professional Growth
- REL012100 RELIGION / Christian Life / Relationships
- REL012110 RELIGION / Christian Life / Social Issues
- REL012120 RELIGION / Christian Life / Spiritual Growth
- REL099000 RELIGION / Christian Life / Spiritual Warfare
- REL063000 RELIGION / Christian Life / Stewardship & Giving
- REL012130 RELIGION / Christian Life / Women's Issues
- RELIGION / Christian Literature see Christianity / Literature & the Arts
- REL109000 RELIGION / Christian Ministry / General
- REL109010 RELIGION / Christian Ministry / Adult

- REL109020 RELIGION / Christian Ministry / Children
- REL050000 RELIGION / Christian Ministry / Counseling & Recovery
- REL023000 RELIGION / Christian Ministry / Discipleship
- REL030000 RELIGION / Christian Ministry / Evangelism
- REL045000 RELIGION / Christian Ministry / Missions
- REL074000 RELIGION / Christian Ministry / Pastoral Resources
- REL080000 RELIGION / Christian Ministry / Preaching
- REL109030 RELIGION / Christian Ministry / Youth
- REL055000 RELIGION / Christian Rituals & Practice / General
- REL055010 RELIGION / Christian Rituals & Practice / Sacraments
- REL055020 RELIGION / Christian Rituals & Practice / Worship & Liturgy
- REL067000 RELIGION / Christian Theology / General
- REL067010 RELIGION / Christian Theology / Angelology & Demonology
- REL067020 RELIGION / Christian Theology / Anthropology
- REL067030 RELIGION / Christian Theology / Apologetics
- REL067040 RELIGION / Christian Theology / Christology
- RELIGION / Christian Theology / Doctrinal see Christian Theology / Systematic
- REL067050 RELIGION / Christian Theology / Ecclesiology
- REL067060 RELIGION / Christian Theology / Eschatology
- REL067070 RELIGION / Christian Theology / Ethics
- REL067080 RELIGION / Christian Theology / History
- REL067120 RELIGION / Christian Theology / Liberation
- REL104000 RELIGION / Christian Theology / Mariology
- REL067090 RELIGION / Christian Theology / Pneumatology
- REL067130 RELIGION / Christian Theology / Process
- REL067100 RELIGION / Christian Theology / Soteriology
- REL067110 RELIGION / Christian Theology / Systematic
- REL070000 RELIGION / Christianity / General
- REL002000 RELIGION / Christianity / Amish
- REL003000 RELIGION / Christianity / Anglican

- REL073000 RELIGION / Christianity / Baptist
- REL093000 RELIGION / Christianity / Calvinist
- REL009000 RELIGION / Christianity / Catechisms
- REL010000 RELIGION / Christianity / Catholic
- REL083000 RELIGION / Christianity / Christian Science
- REL046000 RELIGION / Christianity / Church of Jesus Christ of Latter-day Saints (Mormon)
- RELIGION / Christianity / Congregational see Christianity / United Church of Christ
- REL094000 RELIGION / Christianity / Denominations
- REL027000 RELIGION / Christianity / Episcopalian
- RELIGION / Christianity / Friends see Christianity / Quaker
- REL015000 RELIGION / Christianity / History
- RELIGION / Christianity / Holidays see headings under Holidays
- RELIGION / Christianity / Holy Spirit see Christian Theology / Pneumatology
- REL096000 RELIGION / Christianity / Jehovah's Witnesses
- REL013000 RELIGION / Christianity / Literature & the Arts
- REL082000 RELIGION / Christianity / Lutheran
- REL043000 RELIGION / Christianity / Mennonite
- REL044000 RELIGION / Christianity / Methodist
- RELIGION / Christianity / Mormon see Christianity / Church of Jesus Christ of Latter-day Saints   (Mormon)
- REL049000 RELIGION / Christianity / Orthodox
- REL079000 RELIGION / Christianity / Pentecostal & Charismatic
- RELIGION / Christianity / Prayerbooks see Prayerbooks / Christian
- REL097000 RELIGION / Christianity / Presbyterian
- REL053000 RELIGION / Christianity / Protestant
- REL088000 RELIGION / Christianity / Quaker
- RELIGION / Christianity / Roman Catholic see Christianity / Catholic
- REL110000 RELIGION / Christianity / Saints & Sainthood
- RELIGION / Christianity / Sermons see Sermons / Christian
- REL098000 RELIGION / Christianity / Seventh-Day Adventist

- REL059000 RELIGION / Christianity / Shaker
- RELIGION / Christianity / Society of Friends see Christianity / Quaker
- RELIGION / Christianity / Unitarian Universalism see Unitarian Universalism
- REL111000 RELIGION / Christianity / United Church of Christ
- RELIGION / Church Administration see Christian Church / Administration
- RELIGION / Church & State see Religion, Politics & State
- RELIGION / Church Institutions & Organizations see Institutions & Organizations
- REL081000 RELIGION / Clergy
- REL017000 RELIGION / Comparative Religion
- REL018000 RELIGION / Confucianism
- REL019000 RELIGION / Counseling
- REL020000 RELIGION / Cults
- REL021000 RELIGION / Deism
- REL100000 RELIGION / Demonology & Satanism
- REL022000 RELIGION / Devotional
- RELIGION / Discipleship see Christian Ministry / Discipleship
- REL024000 RELIGION / Eastern
- RELIGION / Ecclesiastical Law see Christian Church / Canon & Ecclesiastical Law
- REL107000 RELIGION / Eckankar
- REL025000 RELIGION / Ecumenism & Interfaith
- REL026000 RELIGION / Education
- REL085000 RELIGION / Eschatology
- REL113000 RELIGION / Essays
- REL028000 RELIGION / Ethics
- REL029000 RELIGION / Ethnic & Tribal
- RELIGION / Evangelism see Christian Ministry / Evangelism
- REL077000 RELIGION / Faith
- RELIGION / Freemasonry see SOCIAL SCIENCE / Freemasonry & Secret Societies
- REL078000 RELIGION / Fundamentalism

- REL112000 RELIGION / Gnosticism
- REL032000 RELIGION / Hinduism / General
- REL032010 RELIGION / Hinduism / History
- REL032020 RELIGION / Hinduism / Rituals & Practice
- REL032030 RELIGION / Hinduism / Sacred Writings
- REL032040 RELIGION / Hinduism / Theology
- REL033000 RELIGION / History
- REL034000 RELIGION / Holidays / General
- REL034010 RELIGION / Holidays / Christian
- REL034020 RELIGION / Holidays / Christmas & Advent
- REL034030 RELIGION / Holidays / Easter & Lent
- REL034040 RELIGION / Holidays / Jewish
- REL034050 RELIGION / Holidays / Other
- RELIGION / I Ching see BODY, MIND & SPIRIT / I Ching
- REL036000 RELIGION / Inspirational
- REL016000 RELIGION / Institutions & Organizations
- REL037000 RELIGION / Islam / General
- REL037010 RELIGION / Islam / History
- REL041000 RELIGION / Islam / Koran & Sacred Writings
- REL037020 RELIGION / Islam / Law
- REL037030 RELIGION / Islam / Rituals & Practice
- REL037040 RELIGION / Islam / Shi'a
- REL090000 RELIGION / Islam / Sufi
- REL037050 RELIGION / Islam / Sunni
- REL037060 RELIGION / Islam / Theology
- REL038000 RELIGION / Jainism
- RELIGION / Jewish Life see Judaism / Rituals & Practice
- REL040000 RELIGION / Judaism / General
- REL040050 RELIGION / Judaism / Conservative
- REL040030 RELIGION / Judaism / History
- RELIGION / Judaism / Holocaust see HISTORY / Holocaust
- REL040060 RELIGION / Judaism / Kabbalah & Mysticism
- REL040070 RELIGION / Judaism / Orthodox

- RELIGION / Judaism / Prayerbooks, Prayers, Liturgy see Prayerbooks / Jewish
- REL040080 RELIGION / Judaism / Reform
- REL040010 RELIGION / Judaism / Rituals & Practice
- REL040040 RELIGION / Judaism / Sacred Writings
- REL064000 RELIGION / Judaism / Talmud
- REL040090 RELIGION / Judaism / Theology
- RELIGION / Koran see Islam / Koran & Sacred Writings
- REL071000 RELIGION / Leadership
- REL042000 RELIGION / Meditations
- REL101000 RELIGION / Messianic Judaism
- REL086000 RELIGION / Monasticism
- RELIGION / Muslim see headings under Islam
- REL047000 RELIGION / Mysticism
- RELIGION / Mythology see SOCIAL SCIENCE / Folklore & Mythology
- REL117000 RELIGION / Paganism & Neo-Paganism
- RELIGION / Pastoral Counseling see Christian Ministry / Counseling & Recovery
- RELIGION / Pastoral Ministry see Christian Ministry / Pastoral Resources
- REL051000 RELIGION / Philosophy
- REL087000 RELIGION / Prayer
- REL052000 RELIGION / Prayerbooks / General
- REL052010 RELIGION / Prayerbooks / Christian
- REL052030 RELIGION / Prayerbooks / Islamic
- REL052020 RELIGION / Prayerbooks / Jewish
- REL075000 RELIGION / Psychology of Religion
- REL054000 RELIGION / Reference
- REL106000 RELIGION / Religion & Science
- REL084000 RELIGION / Religion, Politics & State
- REL116000 RELIGION / Religious Intolerance, Persecution & Conflict
- RELIGION / Rituals & Practice see specific religions

- RELIGION / Rosicrucianism see BODY, MIND & SPIRIT / Hermetism & Rosicrucianism
- RELIGION / Satanism see Demonology & Satanism
- REL089000 RELIGION / Scientology
- REL058000 RELIGION / Sermons / General
- REL058010 RELIGION / Sermons / Christian
- REL058020 RELIGION / Sermons / Jewish
- REL105000 RELIGION / Sexuality & Gender Studies
- REL060000 RELIGION / Shintoism
- REL061000 RELIGION / Sikhism
- RELIGION / Sociology of Religion see SOCIAL SCIENCE / Sociology of Religion
- REL062000 RELIGION / Spirituality
- RELIGION / Stewardship see Christian Life / Stewardship & Giving
- RELIGION / Sufi see Islam / Sufi
- RELIGION / Talmud see Judaism / Talmud
- REL065000 RELIGION / Taoism (see also PHILOSOPHY / Taoist)
- REL066000 RELIGION / Theism
- REL102000 RELIGION / Theology
- REL068000 RELIGION / Theosophy
- REL103000 RELIGION / Unitarian Universalism
- REL118000 RELIGION / Wicca (see also BODY, MIND & SPIRIT / Witchcraft)
- RELIGION / Youth Ministries see Christian Education / Children & Youth
- RELIGION / Zen Buddhism see Buddhism / Zen
- REL069000 RELIGION / Zoroastrianism
- SCIENCE
- SELF-HELP
- SEL000000 SELF-HELP / General
- SEL005000 SELF-HELP / Aging
- SEL036000 SELF-HELP / Anxieties & Phobias
- SELF-HELP / Bereavement see Death, Grief, Bereavement

- sELF-HELP / Chemical Dependence see headings under Substance Abuse & Addictions
- SEL040000 SELF-HELP / Communication & Social Skills
- SEL010000 SELF-HELP / Death, Grief, Bereavement
- SEL012000 SELF-HELP / Dreams
- SEL045000 SELF-HELP / Journaling
- SEL019000 SELF-HELP / Meditations
- SELF-HELP / Memory Improvement see Personal Growth / Memory Improvement
- SEL021000 SELF-HELP / Motivational & Inspirational
- SEL031000 SELF-HELP / Personal Growth / General
- SEL035000 SELF-HELP / Self-Management / Time Management
- SEL032000 SELF-HELP / Spiritual
- SOCIAL SCIENCE
- SPORTS & RECREATION
- STUDY AIDS
- TECHNOLOGY & ENGINEERING
- TRANSPORTATION
- TRAVEL
- TRUE CRIME
- YOUNG ADULT FICTION
- YOUNG ADULT NONFICTION

Disclaimer

This publication is designed to provide condensed information. It is not intended to reprint all the information that is otherwise available, but instead to complement, amplify and supplement other texts. You are urged to read all the available material, learn as much as possible and tailor the information to your individual needs.

Every effort has been made to make this publication as complete and as accurate as possible. However, there may be mistakes, both typographical and in content. Therefore, this text should be used only as a general guide and not as the ultimate source of information.

The purpose of this publication is to educate. The author shall have neither liability nor responsibility to any person or entity with respect to any loss or damage caused, or alleged to have been caused, directly or indirectly, by the information contained in this publication.

You are advised to visit your Amazon accounts for kindle and CreateSpace publishing to check for new and updated categories.

33100491R00081